Things I Think About and Other Works

A Healing Through Creative Expression

Nadia Ramelle

Copyright © 2024 *Things I Think About* by Nadia Ramelle

All rights reserved. This book or any portion thereof may not be reproduced or used in any manner whatsoever without the express written permission of the publisher except for the use of brief quotations in a book review.

Printed in the United States of America

First Printing, 2024

ISBN (print): 979-8-3304-5935-3

ISBN (ebook): 979-8-3304-5936-0

Contents

A Little Intro	vii
During the Documentation of My Existence	1
Aware of the Duplication, I Thought to Myself...	5
I was starved...	7
Dead Ends	8
Wow	9
Home	10
Who is He	25
Noted	26
Se La Vie	27
Who is to blame?	28
Life Change	29
For Country	34
...and a wake up	36
Perfectionism	38
DUI	39
Where do wars and fights come from among you?	40
Awareness	42
Damn	43
So Many Questions	44
Man is Definitely a Marvel	47
Sensitive Soul	49
Compelled by The Should, The Could, The Would	50
A Life Changed	52

Wallowing	55
Avatar	57
A Life so Vain	58
D(omestic) V(iolence)	60
Riots	61
Gift	63
Moral injury	65
A Nervous System Deregulated	67
Acceptance	68
Creating Patterns	69
Becoming Aware	71
Lady Aya	72
Gratitude	74
Salty	75
DMT	77
NOPE	79
Officer Down	80
More Questions	86
What are you waiting for..	89
Divided	92
Accountability	93
Growth	94
Live An Unbelievable Life	95
A Note from the Author	97
About the Author	99

Dedication

Thank you
God
Family
Friends
The Blue
The Green
The Red
The Nurses
The Dispatchers
The EMTs/Paramedics
The Creatives
The Priests, Pastors, and Shamans
West Coast Post Trauma Retreat (WCPR)
Mighty Oaks
Mil-tree
The Deuce Nine and all the desert cities
Lastly,
The 158 & The OPD

A Little Intro

I live life as a Black woman in America.

I spent the better part of a decade serving as a police officer in one of the most dangerous and violent cities in America, in Oakland, California.

My break from this was my one weekend-a-month obligation as an Officer in the United States Army Reserves.

I have been called racist, a white nationalist, bitch, nigger, nigger bitch, difficult, ugly, I have been told my mother hates me...

To name a few.

I have hated and questioned my existence.

I have been depressed, manic, resentful, angry, bitter, and suicidal.

I lived with chronic pain.

A Little Intro

I bore witness to a tremendous and uncommon amount of violence, hate, and rage.

I have witnessed death in a way that is unimaginable.

I have witnessed the unthinkable violations of men, women, children, and animals.

I have seen maimed bodies,

women's teeth pushed through their lips,

burned corpses,

brains leaking from ears,

abused women and children,

sexual assaults of women and children,

dead children, dying at the hands of those who were supposed to love and protect them.

Seeing a dead child in these ways changes something inside of you.

Couple that with the expectation that this was par for the course: working overtime, testifying, handling caseloads, calls for service, dealing with peers, and engaging in politics, all while attempting to maintain some normalcy in my personal life.

And as I was told I chose the careers, I chose the city; that was my cost of doing business,

...deal with it

I have been on a search for an understanding of myself and other humans.

A Little Intro

I am a lifelong learner and curious about all aspects of life.

That curiosity led me to write some thoughts and share some stories.

Enjoy

During the Documentation of My Existence

I realized
I am nothing
I am everything
The high
The low
The in-between
Where death meets life

That There is No End

Without your beginning
You make the choice
So choose wisely
Wisdom is the building block
The foundation of all that is good

If you choose to stay with ignorance
You will surely stay the fool
A fool's folly is often gleeful
But often falls short
Short of what?
You make the choice
As there is no end without your
    beginning
You make the choice

Death is Essential to Living, Just as Breath is to Lungs…

Every beginning must come an end
Every end, starts a beginning
This one stops with me
I am the beginning
I am the ending
Awakened
I stare blankly
Into the abyss
Of that belief of, what,
Matters
I laugh,
For every beginning must come an end
Every end, starts a new beginning

Death and I Became Acquainted, I Wrote to Her…

Death,
Nice to meet your acquaintance,
yet again
I once thought you a foe
Now I realize that foe was always me
Your lessons
Planned perfection
For my enlightenment
Our entanglement
Was for my enlightenment
Your presentation is not for the faint
But you built me
I stand in that strength
Death will always welcome me
My friend,
Till the end

Whimsical She Is…

Death,
She comes and she goes
Where will she stop

Things I Think About and Other Works

    No one knows

With open arms
Welcome her embrace

Aware of the Duplication, I Thought to Myself...

God moves through me
Sun shining so bright
These pen strokes
Like magic
As I write
Who do I write for?
Me?
You?
It is not for either of us
to determine.
Only the reader will know.
For only the writing will show
it is not for me,
Nor for you.
Like magic,

Only the reader will know.
God moves through
These pen strokes.

I was starved...

Sleep again at the wheel I see
Wake up!
You are going to drive off the edge
Fall into the void
Is that where you are choosing to go?
Alright...
Let's take a trip
The the wheel
But you have to wake
Enlighten yourself
Take that path
The one less traveled
It is the only way

Dead Ends

To be fully alive means dead ends are
    not dead
A spiritual death means everyday has a
    dead end,
but everyday is a new beginning
Dead ends should direct your attention
everyday is a divine appointment
Everyday is full of promise

Wow

23 July 2016 changed my life forever
I was not alone in that car; I had the hand of God on me
I have been on the search for the human condition, trying to understand why this man was determined to end my life.
I understand the politics of community and police, but to me, that was not good enough.
That! That was something else.
During my tenure as a police officer, I witnessed a lot of bad and some evil, but to be the sole recipient of pure evil was life-altering.

Home

I have been exploring what home
    means to me.

When I was 9 I remember coming up
    here to 29 palms and seeing this
    <u>LARGE arrangement of lights</u>

<u>wow!</u>

I'm entering the big city look at all
    these lights shining so bright,

then the sun came up. I woke up,
    surrounded by ugly buildings; men
    and a few women dressed in
    uniform.

Nadia Ramelle

Where the hell are we?

As a child I knew THIS wasn't it
How could it be..
My high school graduating class was
 only 100 kids,
not one like me
nothing to do
Nothing to see

But Like my parents, I knew I wanted
 to serve.
You see They were both Devil Dogs:
 For those of you who don't know
 what Devil Dogs are, it means they
 are Marines: oo rah!.
I wanted to help, I wanted to stand out
 and show off, but how?

I knew I wanted to leave this small,
 transient, dusty town

the grass must be greener somewhere
 else . . .

Frankly I just wanted to see some
 damn grass

So I left to sow my seeds , maybe grow
    some grass of my own

leaving my childhood home, the
    familiar, I went North

I landed in the Bay Area
There wasn't a desert in sight
Not a cactus, not a grain of sand
And though it was greener,
Nothing I pursued made me happy.

I went to college, I played hoop,
I was bored out of my mind!
I didn't seem to fit in. I didn't feel at
    home.
It made me wonder why I even left the
    desert

But I'm not a quitter, so I stuck it out
Eventually, I was hanging out in Oakland
The POLICE.
I decided to become the police
Excellent idea, this felt right!
I mean, I'm Black
Oakland is definitely Black

Nadia Ramelle

I will definitely fit in here

Boy, was I naive

Little did I know what hell I was
        signing up for
I was "the man!"
I had to adjust on the fly
I fixed my mouth to say the roughest
        things
I drank with the boys
Slept with the girls
And became a runner and a gunner in
        the streets

I became somebody I didn't recognize
I wore a resting bitch face
I became the quintessential angry
        black woman
with a quick/slick tongue and even
        quicker temper
I was professional, well put together,
        fit

I was a servant to the public
But was this me?

That's the one question I would ask myself,
but I could never find the answer

I definitely did not fit in
And it was definitely not home!

I became horrified, terrified and exhilarated
all at the same time

The poverty, the rage, the violence, the blood, the guts,
the dismissal, the lies, the hurt, the cheating,
the divorces, the suicides, the car chases,
the fights, the riots, the despair, the destruction...

You ever seen a child die?

Every day there was tragedy

One warm April day some asshole pointed a gun at me
So I responded

I pointed mine right back at him
(beat ya!)
I heard the Boom
As I fired one into his chest
I saw my slide rip back
The casing eject
The smoke rise from my firearm
His blood soaked t-shirt,
his green boxers showing
just above his light blue jeans

He dropped

I stood over him
"Sis, Sis why'd you shoot me sis?"
Shocked but calm
Coldly
I reminded him, that if he goes toward
    the machete at his hip
or moves another inch, I'd blow his
    head off

Point... Blank... range

The words left my lips so smooth, I
    meant that shit

After more units showed up, I left the
    scene along with a piece of my
    soul

Later that evening I was met with a
    shot of Jameson and a somber
    "welcome to the club"

I understood I would have to be a soul
    taker

What a defining moment
Yes, it was Justified,
but I was unable to look in the mirror

when I did, I looked as empty as I felt

How could I do that?

I couldn't feel a thing: I felt numb, l
    started floating through the days

At that point I didn't even have a home
    in my body

But I was tough, I was a badass,
    RIGHT?

Feeling soulless
I still stayed, I'm no quitter!
With this unique skill set
No where else to go
Heart shattered
So dissociated

I drank and drank and drank
I mean at least I was a part of a club
RIGHT?
I thought to myself, maybe NOW I am
    home -
I am a part of the few
As this is not a common thing

They say Home is where the heart is,

My ass!

my heart was broken

I became a glutton for punishment
I mean at that point it made more
    sense
to welcome that new feeling of
    disconnect
I mean, What did it matter?

I didn't belong anywhere anyway.

My piece became my peace
My peace was in the chaos
My peace was in guns, fast cars, fast
    relationships,
I did not even have peace in my sleep
My conscience and subconscience
    blurred together
Into lucid nightmares
I once knew the line, that shit had all
    been erased
And I thrived in that

This was my new normal
The chaos
The drama
The trauma
I was making all that my new home

Secretly, I had my doubts
This existence was going to kill me
And probably by my own hand

I was so dissociated
Life and death had no meaning
Death was just a violent part of life

Nadia Ramelle

And Life was meaningless

I was clearly not afraid to die

And to my maker, I said, "Take me, I'm
 ready"

Little did I know my wish was about to
 come true

2016,
my last shift ever
A drunk driver ran a red and t boned
 my patrol vehicle
Drivers side smashed
Front window smashed
Cage in the back
Stuck
Unable to move
ambushed
I saw him standing there at my
 passenger-side window
Time stood still

I could hear each inhale and exhale of
 my breath
I stared into his lifeless/soulless eyes

and he back into mine

I saw the barrel
I heard the gunshots

(Damn — all I could think was "this is
 it, and I sure don't want to die in
 this filthy patrol car")

I felt this separation as if I was about to
 watch my body die

But nothing happened

Then I saw it, the double feed - two
 rounds locked in place

His gun, locked in place, he can't
 shoot me,
(Can he?)

Believe me he tried, over and over and
 over again

As you can see I am standing before
 you today

Nadia Ramelle

Unfortunately the little I had left of my
    soul exploded, splintered and
    floated away - the little bit left of
    my heart had gone into the ether

I broke like the levees in Louisiana

Everything I knew to be true dissolved
All that was left was
Failure
Paranoia
Rage
hate
Mixed in with deep sorrow and
    depression

Can't keep a steady hand
Nervous system shot
Vessel empty
Sleeping with my finger on the trigger
I pray no one has to live like that

Miraculously something in me refused
    to give up
God reminded me, not to give up

I decided to return to the only home I
have ever known.

You know, My parents stayed right
here in the Hi-Desert. They have
always loved me unconditionally,
and their home is safe, comfortable,
familiar.

When I returned
I finally recognized the beauty that I
long ago took for granted
Hell, I did not need any green grass
Turns out, I preferred the sand in my
toes anyway

I preferred The different hue of the
desert sky and tempered weather

And I like to see the sparseness of the
vegetation

Damn, like me they can survive the
harshest environments

Had this been home all along?

Nadia Ramelle

I have to tell you, I have not found that
    home is where heart is

I put my heart and soul into the world
    (that job as a police officer), and I
    lost both
I need to walk wisely
What I need for home to be is
    something different

It needs to be
Safe and Joyful
Where I can be the freest
To be who I am
Full of peace and quiet

Here in the desert
I open my eyes
I look up
I am Surrounded by palm trees and stars
Moonlight and sunrises
Truly an oasis of beauty

I am a work in progress
I am being resurrected
Finding my way

Finally finding my way home

I will leave you with this quote from Rumi:

"Yesterday I was clever, so I wanted to change the world. Today I am wise, so I am changing myself."

Who is He

God draws His patterns in the sky
Miraculous each day
God brings in his beauty upon me
I sit and gaze at the creation
The marvel
The wonder
O is He!
I take pride in being His child
O father
Take mercy on me!

Noted

Trauma is held in the body, in places
    talking will not heal, this is a
    spiritual matter
One that the mind, body and soul need
    to team up and fight like hell to
    find the harmony within

Se La Vie

In order gain
You must be prepared to lose
Preparation is not always adequate
Nor at you beck and call,
Such is life

Who is to blame?

It may not be your fault, but it is your
    problem
You will always know them by their
    fruits
Yourself included.

Life Change

WHAT PROMPTED the biggest change in my life? This was the writing prompt written in chalk on the blackboard as I walked into the classroom.

My immediate thought was, *damn, I just wrote something similar three weeks ago.* I performed and gave testimony to this very time in my life. Disclosing a very vulnerable time where everything I knew was blown to pieces, and I was left high and dry to search for meaning, to search for those parts of me floating in the void.

I then settled on, "hell," I will write something else.

What else, what...else?

I went through an inventory of my life.

What brought me back here?

This brought me back to this very moment, where I

am again exposing myself and expressing the most vulnerable parts of myself.

I guess I can discuss the overarching theme in my life: the loss and search for identity.

So many individual moments.

Near-death experiences, a suicide run-through, hating life, idealized and self-sacrificing relationships, terrible coping skills, self-depreciation, self-loathing, the realization of not knowing myself, mental health issues, isolation, depression, panic attacks, manic episodes, plant medicine trips, community, the Bible...

developing a relationship with God.

Almost all encompassed a focus of identity in all things outside of which I was created.

There is one highlighted and faithful moment that created the biggest change in my life.

That was my discovery through reading the word that God had written to us.

...A love letter...

Although you did not know me, I knew
  you (Psalms 139.1)

I knit you together in your mother's
    womb (Psalms 139.13)
I am familiar with your ways (Psalms
    139.13)
You are my masterpiece (Ephesians
    2:10)
You are fearfully and wonderfully
    made (Psalms 139.14)
Even the hairs on your head are
    numbered (Mathew 10:29-31)
I knew you before you were conceived
    (Jeremiah 1: 4-5)
You are not a mistake, for all your days
    are written in my book (Psalms 139
    15-16)
Again, I knew you before you were
    conceived (Jeremiah 1: 4-5)
You were made in my image (Genesis
    1:27)
I chose you, my desire is to lavish my
    love on you (1 John 4:16)
You are my treasured possession
    (Exodus 19:5)
When you are broken hearted, I am
    close to you (Psalms 34:18)
I will wipe every tear from your eye
    (Revelation 21:4)

> His death was my ultimate expression
> of my love for you (1 John 4:10)
> I gave up everything I love, that I might
> gain your love (Romans 8 31-32)
> I have always been Father, and will
> always be father (Ephesians 3 14-
> 15)
> I am waiting for you (Luke 15 11-12)

With each word spoken aloud, my heart had once again become flesh. Through each trial, tribulation, and agonizing and suffering breath, I realized I was not alone—that my identity was right here all along.

My broken pieces were not in the void but sewn into the heavens.

I can look around and see them illuminated through each waking moment.

The inventory I took of my life revealed that what I thought was my life was never mine to begin with. I realized I was not the author of my life and that every toil was meaningless under the sun.

I know I can say that that love letter pointed me to that pivotal truth, that discovering God's love was the most life-changing event that had ever occurred.

That my identity was that of a child, a child of the most high.

That my identity was tied to love, that agape love;

it is the reason for my breath, these words, and my being here today.

I dare not direct my own steps or pave my own road.

I have learned "that the road to hell is paved with good intentions."

I thought all was good; nothing was further from the truth, as I did not recognize God's love in my life or my identity in the kingdom.

I removed my goddess crown and accepted a different anointing for this life.

"Heavy is the head that wears the crown," it is said, but my dang neck hurts!

I realized there was something greater than physical death and that life without God's love is meaningless, unfruitful, a pointless road leading to nowhere.

That love letter shaped the identity of who you see before you today. It changed the course of my life, and I hope it will change yours as well.

Wow, I can touch Jerusalem from here.

For Country

So many thoughts of ending it all. Why was I alive? Why didn't you just let the bullets fly? What do you want from me, I cried out, why did you spare this life? I have tried, but I am no good, I am low, I am a sinner, wasteful with this gift. What did I do to deserve this chance? I am poor, lowly, angry, bitter, depressed, I bring nothing to this world. I am nothing.

You realize that the thing you signed up for, the protection of life, the protection of property is overruled by an agenda. The agenda of

whom? That I don't really know.
But it for sure ain't the people. It
ain't about life or property.

We serve different masters.

A master of the times. Time is fickle.

Generations come, generations go,
| a great teacher said that

A master of the culture. Culture moves
on a whim.

A master of rights. What rights? The
ones gifted by God?

Or another set of rights set by that of
man based on culture and time?

...and a wake up

My eyes and ears were forcibly opened
> to the reality of not asking such
> questions, relying on feelings, and
> not exploring facts or history. I got
> the brunt of that experience while
> humping calls on the beat, making
> arrests, car chasing, and on one
> occasion, placing someone's
> intestines back into their
> abdomen.

Working in a war zone will do that.

I did not need to go to another country
> to experience this; it is in my
> backyard!

Wake up. I do not mean the wake up or

woke in such a way where it is now
a pejorative.
I mean wake up!
Become woke to what is really going on
around us.
When was the last time you asked
where your hard-earned money
was going after being taxed on the
same dollar?
When was the last time you asked
yourself when and how you have
been impacted by the current state
of affairs, not something you heard
through some form of media?
There is a war in your backyard.

Perfectionism

THE AMERICAN PSYCHOLOGICAL ASSOCIATION defines perfectionism as follows: the tendency to
  demand of others or of oneself an extremely high or even flawless level of performance, in excess of what is required by the situation. It is associated with depression, anxiety, eating disorders, and other mental health problems
  A silent destroyer
  A necessary evil whilst in uniform

DUI

Got the call of a car accident,
two vehicles involved
I ended up arresting one of the drivers
    on suspicion of DUI.
one of my firsts
I took him to the hospital to do a blood
    draw. We spoke, we laughed, and I
    learned a bit about his life
When the court date arrived he never
    showed up, so they postponed it to
    a later date and time. I later found
    out the reason why the case was
    postponed...
he committed suicide
I drank in his honor

Where do wars and fights come from among you?

James 4:1

What is a police - the civil force
What is force?
What is Law Enforcement
What is authority - the right or power
    to give orders, to make decisions, to
    enforce obedience
Who issues authority - those in power,
    those with the authority
You call, I arrive
In a uniform marked with a badge and
    patches, (one if you are from
    Oakland) an American flag.
    Highlighted by the words Police,
    Deputy or Law Enforcement.
This uniform invokes my authority
Again you called me

Nadia Ramelle

I arrive wearing this uniform
A bulletproof vest
Carrying a loaded firearm, extra
    magazines with extra ammunition
A taser
Handcuffs
Batons
What do you think i am there for
You called me
I enforce the law
I protect life
I protect property
I want you to go home
I also want to go home

Sometimes we don't go home
Have you ever heard that bagpipe
    spiritual?
The wail of God's angels returning
    home

I have to answer the call
I took an oath

What about you?

Awareness

Knowing others is intelligence
Knowing yourself is true wisdom

Those who conquer others have force
Those who can control themselves are
    mighty

Those who dare risk death have
    courage
But those who death cannot destroy
    are immortal

        — Tao te Ching Verse 33

Me: Admit I know nothing; it seems to be a proper first step: leaning on my own understanding is for the birds

Damn

I remember laying in that hospital bed,
    vacillating between hysterics,
    crying, shaking, laughing, wanting
    to leave, wanting to stay, wanting to
    sleep, wanting to get up and run
    away as fast as I could while
    everyone stood over me, staring.

I know they just wanted to feel better;
    what in the hell did they just
    witness?

So Many Questions

Who am I,
What am I,
Why do I matter,
Why do I exist,
How do I fit in,
Where do I fit in,
Where is my community,
What am I doing,
What am I doing here,
Why do I have to keep proving myself
    over and over again?
Why am I trying to impress you,
Why does your opinion matter,
Why do they seem happy,
Why am I not just happy,
Why am I jealous,

Nadia Ramelle

Why don't you like me,
Why don't I like me,
Why do you not respect me,
Why do I have to work twice as hard,
Why am I still less than,
Why am I not black enough,
Why are you using me,
Why don't you love me,
Will anyone love me,
Will anyone care for me,
Are they using me,
Am I good enough,
Am I pretty enough,
Do I have enough,
... am I enough?

This is just the short list.

Through the search for the answer to my life question, what I found was that those questions both limited and expanded my view of the world. There is a lot of power in words; words have their own life force, words can take you to the brink, words can take you to ecstasy, they can take you into

different parts of the world,
different parts of your psyche,
words take you anywhere you want
to go.

Words expose your vulnerabilities,
your beliefs, your values, your
strengths, your passions, your
capacity, and how you move
through the world.

For me, those questions I asked were
nothing more than words that
created a story that lived in my
soul,

My script, my movie that I projected
onto the world in the theater of
my life

My own creation

I was the artist, the actress, the
backdrop was my surroundings,
and the extras were every living
soul walking around.

Man is Definitely a Marvel

The Book - hermetica - man is a marvel - ch 11, pg 69

But only human beings possess the
    power of Mind, with which we can
    contemplate the Cosmos and come
    to know God.
Human beings are the meeting place of
    spirit and matter. We have,
    therefore, a dual nature. We are the
    mind, which is enclosed by a
    physical body. The human mind is
    an image of God's Mind — it is
    immortal, eternal, divine, and free.

Me: Well hell, best to get my affairs in order and set my mind on things above.

Sensitive Soul

My gift of sensitivity has often felt like
    a curse because I have taken it for
    granted and been taken advantage
    of...

I have walked into the lion's den
    voluntarily. I have reaped coals
    over my backside in order to feel
    even a small amount of pleasure.

All of it feels cursed, but I made the
    move anyway,

you only live once, right? (YOLO!)

Compelled by The Should, The Could, The Would

In August of 2023, I sat out on a road trip across several states with no plan and no understanding of what kind of adventure I would be embarking on. I just went. I got in my car and drove. Little did I know that my whole world would be opened in a way I never believed imaginable

I had these ideas and expectations resting on my crown, and I thought I needed to be all the things to all the people. It turned out I just needed to be me. It turned out that was the biggest question of all: who was I?

> Who was I without all the should
>   haves?
> Who was I without all the would
>   haves?

Who was I without all the could haves?

Those three statements—the should, the could, and the would—placed unbelievable limitations on my life. Everyone around me had a dream for me, wishes for me, and expectations, but I had none for myself. I trapped myself in my own prison of false beliefs, perceptions, and opinions of others, so much so that when I was freed by the road, I could feel the institutionalization (of my own doing) coursing through my body.

I felt an unraveling, a purge, if you will, of all that tapered me and imprisoned me. All that I had attached myself to or become attached to began to sparate and fall off in the wind.

Those three statements are compelling.

A Life Changed

I WAS WALKING down Broadway one evening, a busy sort of night, shows everywhere. I was dressed down, acting as if I was a civilian, I was like everybody else for the evening. Until I heard it, that unfamiliar male voice called out my last name and my authoritative title.. Officer Clark, Officer Clark I was heading to a show at the Paramount theater when I heard an unfamiliar male voice call out, Officer Clark, Officer Clark. The next thing I know a light skinned black male walked up on me. Approaching me from the front still calling out my last name and title, Officer Clark.

I stopped dead in my tracks. There was a tone in his voice, I was unable to discern which way this tone was heading. Were we about to engage in a gunfight, a fist fight or was he going to hug me. The vacillating thought was very provoking. I felt my body heat up, my eyes widen. This male, how does he know me? I can't place him, who is this? Is he a threat?

I did not not initially respond. He then says, do you remember me, his tone aggressive but his body language said otherside. I told him straight up, No, I am sorry. He proceeded to tell me that I had him arrested. I was working undercover facilitating a drug deal and he was a drug user that was going to help me out. The uniforms came in and he was surrounded by blue and he was carted off into the night.

He said that night changed his life, I changed his life. That arrest led to his coming off of all drugs. And it was because of my efforts. He knew he had to change his life. As he had hit rock bottom. His voice had softened and his eyes began to wield up with tears. Nothing fell, but you can see the emotion in our contact. He was relieved. He was a new man. I let him finish his story and I too could feel the emotion in my chest, the fear seeping away.

This is Why! This is Why!

The reminder hit me, this is why i serve, this is why i was doing what i was doing. The nightmares are okay, the drinking was okay, because I saved another soul, I saved a life. It was not a regular occurrence to be thanked.

This man extended his hand, wanted to shake mine. As I extended my hand in gratitude he asked for a hug and I obliged.

This is why I put it all on the line, this is why the sacrifice, this is why I serve!

Wallowing

Anger, grief, sorrow, rage, resentment,
 with intensity I harbored/carried
 them all;
my heart ached.
I questioned my goodness, my sanity.
My soul was taxed, whooped, and
 burned the hell out.
Why not just end it?
Why does/did any of it matter?
No one was going to love me; no one
 was going to respect me.
I did not matter, especially to myself.
I was reluctant to search for help.
I stayed silent; no one understands me
 anyway.
No one cares to.

Filled with resentment, I continued my
    suffering silently, alone.
Fake smiles
Determined not to be a burden to
    anyone,
I will not allow another to touch this
    pain—
This life-altering suicidal inducing
    pain.
My heart, my body, my spirit, my soul,
broken

Avatar

Me: Sometimes I think of myself as an
   Avatar, a character in a film, I come
   with personalities, emotions, skin
   tones. I really gotta learn to control
   this avatar - learn the ins and outs
   of you

Also me: I gotta stop smoking so
   much weed

A Life so Vain

"Vanity of vanities," says the Preacher;
"Vanity of vanities, all is vanity."
The author writes to begin the book of Ecclesiastes (Ecc), and it is how I understand my own life. All that I had thought I accomplished was vanity; my service was vanity.
According to multiple dictionaries, I compiled a list of what vanity means.
Vanity is inflated pride in oneself, something that is empty or valueless, a quality of being useless or futile.
The author continues;

*"What profit has a man from all his labor
In which he toils under the sun?"* (Ecc 1:3 NKJV)
As did my own question;
What did I profit from my labors under the sun? Pain, anguish, struggle, money, madness, power, respect, loneliness, disdain, rage, jadedness, depression, lust, and hate. I could go on, but the list would take up the rest of these pages.
I had no clue who I was or why I did the things that I did. The only thing I had ever really done was toil under the sun.

D(omestic) V(iolence)

The amount of domestic violence is
 staggering, women/women,
 men/men, women/men,
 men/women it did not seem to
 matter the combination.
A display of love, or the reality of the
 human condition?

Riots

Year after year I watched as Oakland
 became what felt like the riot hub
 of this country.
Pallets of bricks, trucks filled with
 shields and makeshift weapons and
 Molotov cocktails, blocking
 freeways, lighting fires, bottles of
 paint mixed with urine, and
 whatever else makes that splatter
 of blue hue.
Each year new reasons for hating law
 and order developed and were
 poured out into the Oakland
 Streets. The wake of these riots left
 mounds of destruction and
 devastation to the small business

owners. Eventually they were forced to move out and large corporations moved in and set up shop.

The bleeding of both bodies and small businesses was epic.

It was all very violent and terrifying. It seemed as if there was a void that needed to be accessed through this destruction. There never really seemed to be any conviction behind the madness. Promises went unfulfilled.

A lot of money was spent.

There was never any reconciliation, just consistent escalation. It was eerie to witness. The seams of the city were slowly, methodically, year after year appearing to be ripping open and lawlessness was beginning to spill out.

Everyone suffered.

Gift

You gifted me another day.
Another day to find my meaning
Another day to expand
Enlighten
And journey into the next chapter of
    my soul's desires
God is with me
I welcome His embrace
He is so gentle
So gentle
Allowing me to take small steps
This day is so hard
But so lovely
As the sun touched my skin
I felt my inside light.
Another day

Another beautiful meaning
My expansion is mighty.
I feel the earth vibrating.
Higher, higher I reach
All my ego crumbled underneath me.
Providing a pedestal, another step
I can almost touch my glory.
It awaits me
This gift, this day, this enlightenment
My soul thanks you.

Moral injury

Loss of meaning,
I felt worthless.
I was unable to look in the mirror; my values, principles, and integrity were gone.
I gained major feelings of guilt and shame and began to distrust everything, every motive, every nice word, everyone.
I began to emotionally distance myself from everyone and withdraw from all forms of communication. I did not feel worthy; I felt like a burden to all, and I wished my life ended that night.
I entered into a practice of self-

> sabotage and harm. The
> cumulative stress, derivative stress,
> and critical incidences had caught
> up to me and broke me.

My life's work—the blood, sweat, and
> tears—held no candle to all the
> unearthed shame, low self-esteem,
> and broken moral compass. I
> reached out to anything that would
> give me attention and fill all the
> empty voids in my life.

Adrenaline was my top three vices.

Anything, anyone, anytime, anywhere.

A Nervous System Deregulated

The nervous system is a complex,
    intelligent communication center
    of the body
Every cell is alive
The years of being exposed to trauma,
    the experience of my own near
    death, had sent my nervous system
    to its breaking point.
Damn, I am burnt the hell out!

Acceptance

I felt like a stranger in my body, and, of
    course, I did not want to look in the
    mirror;
I had physically, mentally, and
    emotionally become a shell of a
    human. I was suffering to live and
    living to suffer.
I was ready to take back my mind, my
    body, and my soul. I refused to
    keep doing the same thing! I had to
    change my life.
I accepted that maybe I was not as in
    control as I originally thought
    I was.

Creating Patterns

In an attempt to understand and chill
 the hell out; our mind creates
 patterns/programs that help us
 "cope".

The sub-conscience mind relies on
 patterns to survive, it appears to be
 highly primal and exists
 somewhere else;

Where? I have no idea, but it is not of
 this world.

Whereas the conscience mind is what
 you experience in every waking
 moment

Both working in tandem, both have
    different functions

The more I think about, the less I have
    a clue

Becoming Aware

Awareness is a true healer
Become critical of your thoughts and
 motives, become introspective
Recognize the lies you tell-!
-you lie to yourself, you will lie to
 others
Hold your thoughts captive!
Gain control
Find the root
Find the rot
Pray

Lady Aya

I was sitting in front of the shaman,
    eyes closed, my body shifting with
    the sound of her voice as she sang
    the icaros.
These prayers entered through my
    ears, eyes, and skin and permeated
    every part of my being. Sage and
    palo santo filled the room and my
    nostrils; the stench was quite
    potent and cleansing at the same
    time.
As the lady shaman concluded, the
    room fell silent, and she handed
    me a cup slightly larger than a shot
    glass.
You could smell the heaviness lurking

inside the cup. I stared into this dark sludge, and it stared back at me, enticing me to drink her.

Lady Ayahuasca called me to take a sip; the shaman called me to take the sip.

I hesitated as I stated my intentions and said a prayer in my cup. The shaman gently tipped my cup toward my mouth.

I placed my mouth on the cup and tipped her back, down my throat she went...

I never returned

Gratitude

I realized through each trial, each
>tribulation, each agonizing and
>suffering breath, I was not alone.

My identity was right here all along.

My broken pieces were not in the void,
>but sewn into the heavens.

I can look around and see them
>illuminated through each waking
>moment.

Salty

One day, I was sitting alone,
tears streaming down my face,
staring back into the memories of my
    old life,
longing for a part of it to return, to
    somehow complete me.
Mixed in that longing were the demons
    of doubt, the demons of the
    shoulda coulda woulda.

The story of Lot's wife became front
    and center of my focus.

Like the title of a movie, the words,

> "but Lot's wife looked back, and she became a pillar of salt" (Genesis 19:26)

DMT

DMT
said to me
God is here, right here with me.
Guarding my feet,
Reminding me I do not have to be
    perfect in His eyes.
I was not created to be anything else
    other than His.
He knows my heart,
I may not get it right, but with Him,
I am never wrong.
My path has been ignited and
    illuminated,
All I have to do is walk
Right into His arms

While I hold my head up high
And be good to my neighbor
And last but not least – love myself.

NOPE

God took all my plans, laughed
said NOPE
Flat out,
Draw 8
Skip
no chance,
pass Go,
do not collect $200

Officer Down

"Code 33! Code 33! - suspect is southbound through the yards."

Officer Taylor, out of breath, alerts the dispatcher over his hand radio.

This thing is like a brick; it can be used as a weapon if needed.

The feedback scorches the airway just as Taylor finishes his direction.

More units are coming onto the radio asking for updates.

Then...SILENCE.

"Where are you, Taylor?" the watch commander asked calmly but sternly.

Five minutes have passed, and still no update from Officer Taylor.

Dispatch is alerted to a fight in the rear yard

behind Miss Johnson's house.

There was one officer and one man dressed in all black—a black watch cap, a black hoodie, and black jeans—and armed with a black gun.

What's the location?

A notoriously violent, drug and gang-infested portion of the city.

Many are held captive by the infestation.

The whirling of the helicopter rages above, shining a spotlight over the area, all in search of Officer Taylor.

SILENCE.

Still nothing.

Officers from around the city are flooding the area.

Officers from surrounding cities chime in over the radio and ask to be of assistance.

SHOTS FIRED…SHOTS FIRED

The helicopter pilot, terrified and choked back by tears, announces over the loudspeaker of his aircraft.

"Officer down, Officer down."

Officer Taylor is lying in a supine position.

His eyes are wide open.

A gaping wound over his right eye,

His mouth is coughing up that bright red arterial blood.

The blood, as he coughs, forms a spray and trickles down onto his face.

He is struggling to breathe, gulping like a fish.

There are holes covering his body.

Blood is pouring out of each hole as if each represents a faucet.

The toucanets are not enough.

Officer Taylor continues to bleed.

Heavy is the head that wears the crown.

And heavy is the blood flow that is leaving Taylor's body.

The arriving officers panicked.

Some yelling.

Some crying.

Some unable to move.

Throw and Go! Throw and Go!

We need to get him to the hospital NOW!

Officers lift Taylor by the legs, arms, and head and carry him to a nearby Black SUV driven by the watch commander.

Each officer and Taylor pile into the back.

Once inside, the watch commander speeds away.

"What are y'all doing?" Officer Taylor asks, confused.

No one seems to bat an eye or look in direction.

Many are shouting,

"TAYLOR, TAYLOR, stay with us.

We are right here, right with you."

TAYLOR, TAYLOR

We are right here, right with you."

As the watch commander pulls into the driveway, the emergency doors open, and a gurney awaits.

"Is that for me?"Taylor asked, confused.

No one looks his way.

The officer removed Taylor from the SUV and placed him on the gurney.

The surrounding nurses and doctors roll Taylor in frantically while all shouting medical jargon.

Everyone is frantic; there is no poise in the room.

There are shook faces everywhere, no one seems to know what to say or how to behave.

Taylor then sees it.

Taylor sees himself lying on the gurney.

Taylor sees his blood-soaked uniform.

Taylor watches as the blood seeps into the pure white sheets of the gurney and onto the tiles of the hospital floor.

"O" - (Taylor)

Taylor realizes that he is staring at himself and not in a mirror but approaching death.

"Well damn" - (Taylor)

"He got me" (Taylor)

SILENCE

All Taylor can hear now is his own breath as he is watching in slow motion his lifeless body, the nurse sitting on his chest providing compressions, the doctors checking vitals and plugging up wounds and refilling the wounds with bags of blood.

The watch commander walks up and stands beside Taylor.

Taylor says: I guess Queen was right; another one bites the dust.

The watch commander chuckles,

"I guess so, son."

The watch commander places his arm around Taylor's shoulder.

Taylor turns toward him, and as he looks at the Watch commander, he notices that his uniform is all white and decorated with halos and pins of the saints.

The two begin to walk off together.

Taylor asks the watch commander, "Have you been supervising me this entire time?"

The watch commander tells Taylor gently, "I have always had your 6."

Taylor asked, "Did you see me hit himwith that brick of a radio?"

Watch Commander replied, "I saw it."

Taylor chuckled.

The Watch Commander said, "Time to go, son, your heart no longer has to be troubled. (John 14:1)

There is a city prepared for you (Hebrews 11:16); a new heaven and a new earth await you.

You did good, my good and faithful servant." (Matthew 25:23)

The two turned, and the whirl of a helicopter and a white spotlight captured them both as they descended into the void.

More Questions

Have you ever wondered what
 thoughts are, or where or how they
 originated?

Have you ever wondered why your
 body is designed in such a way, or
 why it functions in the way that it
 does?

Have you ever wondered about the
 existence and the necessity of the
 soul?

Have you ever wondered why one
 minute you can be feeling so much

happiness and within a few
moments be on the opposite end
and be angry?

Have you ever wondered why you do
    the things you do?

Why was I exposed to so much hate
    and violence?

Why can't we just love and respect
    each other?

Why don't we love and respect God?

Why is there racism, sexism, all the
    isms?

Why is there so much hate?

How did all this originate?

Why did it originate?

What is life?
Why did the cop pull the trigger?

Things I Think About and Other Works

Why are we always at war?
Why so much drug addiction?
Why so much homelessness?
Why so many taxes?
Why are bills 5000 pages?
What is going on?

What are you waiting for..

Take that trip
Write that book
Start that business
Live your life
Why are you allowing others to tell you
    who you are? What you are? And
    why you exist!
Chase your dreams!
You want something different
Do something different!
Commit
Discipline
Love
Get out your comfort zone
Burn that bridge
Do that play

Paint that picture
Don't look back
How bad do you want it!
Don't look back
How bad do you want it!
Where do you wanna go
Who do you want to become
Who are you inspired by
Be an inspiration.
Don't let you hold you back
It's only you vs you
Break the chain
Do more
Be more
Be better
Little by little
Brick by brick
Forget the noise
Be healthy
Be wealth
Believe in yourself
Tell yourself:
I am the best
I am great
I am worthy
I am beautiful
Look in the mirror and tell yourself

Nadia Ramelle

I LOVE YOU!
Be Bold
Be Strong
Be You
DO NOT QUIT!

Divided

A house divided cannot stand -
Matthew 12:22-28
Your mind, body and soul cannot be
 divided, you will not stand.
A people divided cannot stand
Those who don't learn from history are
 doomed to repeat it
Or is it
History doesn't repeat itself, but it sure
 as hell does rhyme

Accountability

Get to know your body
Get to know your mind
Get to know your soul

Growth

Understand that in order to grow, there will ALWAYS have to be the belief in something greater. That is the only way to reach new heights. You hear the greats, the gurus, athletes, thought leaders, preachers, rabbis, and shamans discussing this mindset. You have the free will, the choice to make whatever decision you want.

What I have learned is when you choose to make yourself the center of your life;

heavy is the head that wears the crown.

Live An Unbelievable Life

The crash and burn that is internally
 embodied when facing trauma can
 kill even the smallest gratitudes of
 life. When you learn to navigate
 trauma it feels as if you
 accomplished the unbelievable.
 Once you accomplish the
 unbelievable, that ability to live the
 unbelievable becomes a reality.
Aim high.
Aim to become the best version of
 yourself, moment by moment,
 incrementally
Sometimes, we fall, you gotta get back
 up again
and again!

Choose grace, choose hope, choose humility, choose peace, choose prayer,
choose your hard!
Forgive yourself so you can then forgive others.
Life will never look the way you think. Expectations, dreams, and goals are what we tell ourselves to achieve, what we believe is the next step. Often, those expectations are based on others' beliefs and the limiting one(s) you have already placed on yourself.
"If you want to make God laugh, tell Him your plans."
Take your time, enjoy the journey, connect with something higher than you, keep learning, keep growing, just keep going.
Blessed be the (wo)man who can learn the lessons of others
Jeremiah 29:11: For I know the plans I have for you

A Note from the Author

From she who wrestles with God, thank you.

In the name of the Father, the Son, and the Holy Spirit,

Amen

Heal Through Your Creative Expression

You can follow me here:
https://www.instagram.com/nadiaramelle/

NADIARAMELLE

About the Author

Nadia Clark has never been one for labels. From collegiate athlete to Police Officer and Army officer, her life has followed many paths, each marked by its own uniform. Now, she has returned to the desert where she grew up, searching for the peace she's always longed for. Though she has always been an artist at heart, her creativity has been something she has kept to herself—until now. Nadia is ready to share her journey, offering a unique perspective through her art.

Printed in the USA
CPSIA information can be obtained
at www.ICGtesting.com
CBHW031628251024
16402CB00017B/281